A Guided Journey to Your Authentic Self

How to write the highest vibrating, most powerful affirmations to manifest love, positivity, peace, self-confidence, motivation, success, and other wonderful things

FREE GIFT

To get the best experience from this book,
I created beautiful, soothing, phone screen
affirmational wallpaper just for you.

Be reminded of your affirmational goals
every time you look at your phone!
They work on all phones.

I invite you to download them here:
toolbox.dianemetcalf.com/freeaffirmations

FREE
THE TOOLBOX APP
Instant information, support, and validation as you recover and
move on from narcissistic, dysfunctional, hurtful, or toxic
relationships.

Google Play: https://bit.ly/3361PWD
App Store: https://apple.co/3hxrivM

I appreciate you!

Words Matter

> Written words, spoken words, they all matter. It matters what others say to you and it matters what you say to yourself.

A combination of negative self-talk and limiting beliefs can keep you stuck.

Have you ever really observed how you talk to yourself? Some of us are not very nice to ourselves, and others are just plain abusive. What kinds of things do you say to yourself? Is your self-talk positive and loving? Do you beat yourself up and tell yourself hurtful things?

What we tell ourselves is linked to how we feel. Changing your self-talk from an unsupportive inner dialogue to an uplifting and proactive one brings about positive change. If you beat yourself up for perceived failures or shortcomings, how does that help? Does it motivate you to change?

What we tell ourselves isn't only a description of what we believe about ourselves; it is a **command**. Your self-talk TELLS your mind what to think about you! When you tell yourself, "this is just who I am," "I've always been _____," or "I've always done _____," it implies that there's no room for change. These statements tell your brain, "this is it. This is final. There is no more." Why would you want to do that?

.

Affirmational Therapy

The "Law of Attraction" is a viewpoint that suggests thinking positive thoughts can bring about positive effects, and holding negative thoughts can bring adverse outcomes. This law is based on the belief that thoughts are a form of energy, therefore, positive thoughts attract positive energy and vice versa.

Since everything in existence is made of constantly moving elements, atoms and their sub-particles, all things vibrate and create energy. Everything, including the human body, is an energy field. So, everything in existence, including us humans, vibrates at particular frequencies and creates energy. (Srinivasan 2010.)

There's growing evidence that our body's own electrical and magnetic energy can stimulate chemical processes that influence our health and wellbeing. "Vibrational medicine," also called energy medicine, strives to use the energy generated by and around a person's body to optimize their health.

Our vibrations shift according to our physical and mental health, moods, and the energy surrounding us.

Focusing on that which brings us joy and happiness raises our vibrational frequency. When we get ourselves into a higher vibration, we let go of that which no longer serves us. By repeating highly vibrating affirmations regularly, we raise our vibrational frequency.

When you begin releasing everything that weighs you down and you maintain a higher vibration, you will experience more positive emotions. Feeling good will be your default state of being.

Feelings are the Conscious Awareness of Your Vibrational State

Abraham-Hicks, an American author, and speaker on the subject of the Law of Attraction created this "Emotional Guidance Scale," ranked from highest to lowest-vibrating feelings. As you can see, joy and love are among the highest!

- Joy/appreciation/empowerment/freedom/love
- Passion
- Enthusiasm/eagerness/happiness
- Positive expectations/belief
- Optimism
- Hopefulness
- Contentment
- Boredom
- Pessimism
- Frustration/irritation/impatience
- Overwhelm
- Disappointment
- Doubt
- Worry
- Blame
- Discouragement
- Anger
- Revenge
- Hatred/rage
- Jealousy
- Insecurity/guilt/unworthiness
- Fear/grief/depression/despair/powerlessness

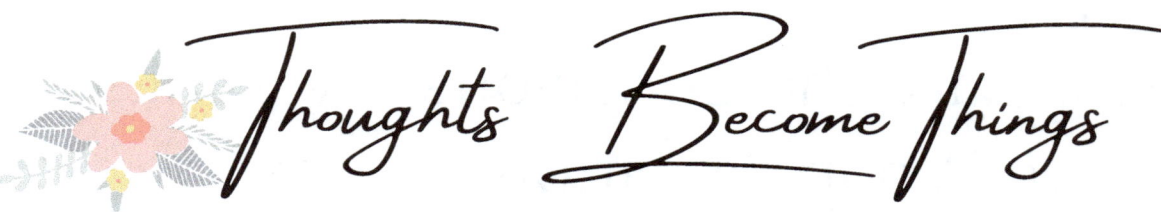

Thoughts Become Things

~We can choose to vibrate higher or lower than our current state of being~

Affirmations can raise your vibration when you're stuck in a low vibrational pattern like fear, worry, anxiety, doubt, and powerlessness. They are a powerful tool for manifesting change and lifting your attitude simultaneously. Speaking well-written, highly vibrating positive affirmations is one of the quickest ways to raise your vibration!

As you continue to use affirmations, your vibration will increase, and you'll notice that you feel happier and more peaceful. You'll begin to attain your goals, fulfill your desires, and attract the people and experiences you want.

Affirmations work to remind us of our highest potential.

When we hold low-vibrational thoughts, feelings, and beliefs, we lower our vibration, inevitably hampering our affirmation's likelihood of success. This is because the subconscious mind accepts *any repeated declaration as truth*.

To manifest your best life, you must raise your vibration to align with your goals. How do you raise your vibration? By speaking strong, highly vibrating affirmations along with implementing the four fundamentals in this book.

Highly vibrating affirmations attract what we've always wanted but believed we couldn't have. As you repeat your affirmations your vibration will increase, and you will begin living in alignment with the life you envision. You will begin attracting like-vibrating people and opportunities.

If your affirmations don't vibrate highly, you must rewrite them until they do.

Create Your New Life

Affirmations are designed to promote an optimistic mindset; they have been shown to reduce the tendency to dwell on negative experiences (Wiesenfeld et al., 2001.) Optimism is a powerful tool! When we replace negative thoughts with positive ones, we are creating a whole new narrative around "who we are" and what we can accomplish.

To achieve the life you want, you will need to write robust, highly vibrating affirmations and believe them to already be true. If you don't write them correctly, you will be wasting your time.

Affirmations that work best are:

- **short:** "I am," "I easily," "I happily." These are short, assertive statements. Avoid "I feel" because feelings are temporary. When you say "I am" it implies permanency. It says **you own it!**

- **clear:** know *exactly* what you want to achieve or change about yourself. This takes reflection, asking yourself tough questions, and honesty.

- **concrete:** use descriptors that show you're *already at the highest level* of achievement, with no room for improvement. For example: "I eagerly embrace all that my life offers" rather than "I love my life."

- **positive:** negative words like "not" and "can't" must be avoided. Instead of **"I am not afraid,"** which focuses on fear, say**"I am brave"** and put your focus *on the outcome you want (bravery.)*

- **present tense:** the higher self works in the present moment!

- **personal:** focus solely on *yourself and your life.*

Three for Each

My friend, Ellen MaRee, Intuitive Life Coach (EllenMaree.com,) teaches people how to integrate with their authentic selves. She advises writing and saying affirmations in sets of three, increasing each affirmation's vibration in turn.

The affirmations below increase in vibration from first to last. An affirmation's *strength and effectiveness increase as its vibration increases.* Soon, *your* vibration will begin to align with your affirmation's vibration as well!

For example, to cultivate a worry-free, peaceful life:

1. I am content and enjoy my life. (Good)
2. I cheerfully cultivate inner peacefulness and gratitude. (Better)
3. I am ceaselessly connected to the infinite, ancient wisdom of the universe and I am lovingly provided with everything that I need or want. (Best)

The first affirmation is acceptable. It's short, clear, concrete, positive, present tense, and personal. It will work. It vibrates nicely.

The second one is stronger because of the added adjective "cheerfully," which is a feeling. *Affirmations should be feeling statements.* Do you feel the difference between numbers one and two?

The third affirmation vibrates very highly; it's short, clear, concrete, positive, present tense, and personal. It has the additional benefit of using adjectives that *describe the highest level of achievement possible.*

As you say this set of three, you should feel **your** vibration increasing with each one. *This is what you want!* You will learn to raise your vibration easily this way with practice.

Four Fundamentals

~Affirmations have the most substantial impact when used frequently and regularly~

Ellen MaRee also advises applying these four fundamentals to your daily practice:

INTEND

When you are intentional, you focus on the present moment. Why do you feel the need to use this particular affirmation? The answer will inform you about your intention. "Receiving" what you are asking for should always be one of your intentions.

AFFIRM

When you speak your affirmations, you declare and validate who you are when living as your authentic self. Speak clearly, assertively, and feel the truth of your statements. **If they don't ring true, re-write them until they do!**

ASK

When you're done speaking your affirmations, it's time to ask for and visualize the things which will contribute to your becoming your authentic self. These include your authentic self's character traits, morals, and skills. Make a list of the personality traits, moral convictions, beliefs, activities that fulfill you, and skills you desire.

EXPRESS GRATITUDE

You've stated your intention and spoken your affirmations in a clear, assertive voice, basking in their truth, and increasing your vibration. You've asked for and visualized the changes you want to make. Now **thank your higher power** for helping you to connect with your authentic self and creating the life you desire.

When starting a new practice like self-affirmation, it's important to make your affirmations easily accessible to help build the daily habit of saying them. Keep them where they're convenient to use.

Many people keep them on their phones because they're usually within reach. Some set reminders or alarms for speaking them at certain times. Others like to write their affirmations in a journal or notebook and read them silently. Some write their affirmations on index cards or sticky notes and leave them in places they'll notice at particular times throughout the day.

Affirmations can also be used as writing prompts; as you think about each affirmation, journal about the thoughts and feelings that arise.

Speaking affirmations aloud is an effective technique for learning to use your voice as a form of empowerment and self-validation.

This workbook provides the ability to save your affirmations here or to use them as prompts for journaling or cut them out and physically keep them elsewhere. I invite you to write your affirmations in the dedicated space at the back of the book, as groups of three, in increasing vibrational frequency (good, better, best.) Cut them out, fold them, and keep them in a bowl or box made of a natural element. Natural elements like glass, crystal, timber, and even large shells add positive vibrations of their own.

Each morning choose one of the folded slips and speak the three affirmations aloud several times throughout the day.

A journey to loving myself

I'm here
I'm alive
I'm grateful
I'm ready

MY VALUES

Love / Purpose / Self Care
Creativity / Community / Friendship

SPIRITUAL SELF CARE

EMOTIONAL SELF CARE

....

♡

....

physical
self
care

I stand in my truth,
and
I am heard

SOCIAL SELF CARE

Begin with Intentions

What I want to change:

♡

♡

♡

♡

♡

♡

♡

What I want to accomplish:

Characteristics of my authentic self:

My Intentions

What I want to change:

What I want to accomplish:

♡

♡

♡

♡

♡

♡

♡

♡

Characteristics of my authentic self:

# My Intentions

What I want to change:

♡

♡

♡

♡

♡

♡

♡

What I want to accomplish:

Characteristics of my authentic self:

My Intentions

What I want to change:

What I want to accomplish:

♡
♡
♡
♡
♡
♡
♡
♡

Characteristics of my authentic self:

My Work

thoughts + feelings = beliefs

3 THOUGHTS ABOUT MYSELF THAT I WANT TO CHANGE

♡ _____

♡ _____

♡ _____

3 FEELINGS ABOUT MYSELF THAT I WANT TO CHANGE

♡ _____

♡ _____

♡ _____

3 BELIEFS ABOUT MYSELF THAT I WANT TO CHANGE

♡ _____

♡ _____

♡ _____

Positive Affirmations

ONLY I
CAN DETERMINE
MY SELF-WORTH

I can do hard things

MY RELATIONSHIPS
ARE RESPECTFUL
AND PEACEFUL

I am grateful for all of the love that is in my life.

I LET GO OF THE
NEED FOR
OTHERS TO
VALIDATE ME

I release everything that does not promote positivity in my life

I AM CONNECTED TO THE INFINITE, ANCIENT, WISDOM OF THE UNIVERSE

Write an Affirmation Set

WRITE THE FIRST THOUGHT THAT YOU WANT TO CHANGE:

_____

_____

_____

RE-WRITE THE ABOVE STATEMENT WITH MORE POSITIVITY HERE:

(GOOD) _____

_____

_____

DOES YOUR REWRITTEN STATEMENT CONTAIN WORDS LIKE "NOT" OR "I FEEL?" RE-WRITE IT WITHOUT THOSE HERE:

(BETTER) _____

_____

_____

ADD ADJECTIVES AND FEELINGS TO MAKE IT EVEN STRONGER:

_____

_____

_____

RE-WRITE IT ONCE MORE SO IT IS THE HIGHEST LEVEL OF ACHIEVEMENT POSSIBLE:

(BEST) _____

_____

_____

Write an Affirmation Set

WRITE THE SECOND THOUGHT THAT YOU WANT TO CHANGE:

_____

_____

_____

RE-WRITE THE ABOVE STATEMENT WITH MORE POSITIVITY HERE:

(GOOD) _____

_____

_____

DOES YOUR REWRITTEN STATEMENT CONTAIN WORDS LIKE "NOT" OR "I FEEL?" RE-WRITE IT WITHOUT THOSE HERE:

(BETTER) _____

_____

_____

ADD ADJECTIVES AND FEELINGS TO MAKE IT EVEN STRONGER:

_____

_____

_____

RE-WRITE IT ONCE MORE SO IT IS THE HIGHEST LEVEL OF ACHIEVEMENT POSSIBLE:

(BEST) _____

_____

_____

Write an Affirmation Set

WRITE THE THIRD THOUGHT THAT YOU WANT TO CHANGE:

_____

_____

_____

RE-WRITE THE ABOVE STATEMENT WITH MORE POSITIVITY HERE:

(GOOD) _____

_____

_____

DOES YOUR REWRITTEN STATEMENT CONTAIN WORDS LIKE "NOT"
OR "I FEEL?" RE-WRITE IT WITHOUT THOSE HERE:

(BETTER) _____

_____

_____

ADD ADJECTIVES AND FEELINGS TO MAKE IT EVEN STRONGER:

_____

_____

_____

RE-WRITE IT ONCE MORE SO IT IS THE HIGHEST LEVEL OF
ACHIEVEMENT POSSIBLE:

(BEST) _____

_____

_____

Write an Affirmation Set

WRITE THE FIRST FEELING THAT YOU WANT TO CHANGE:

_____

_____

_____

RE-WRITE THE ABOVE STATEMENT WITH MORE POSITIVITY HERE:

(GOOD) _____

_____

_____

DOES YOUR REWRITTEN STATEMENT CONTAIN WORDS LIKE "NOT" OR "I FEEL?" RE-WRITE IT WITHOUT THOSE HERE:

(BETTER) _____

_____

_____

ADD ADJECTIVES AND FEELINGS TO MAKE IT EVEN STRONGER:

_____

_____

_____

RE-WRITE IT ONCE MORE SO IT IS THE HIGHEST LEVEL OF ACHIEVEMENT POSSIBLE:

(BEST) _____

_____

_____

Write an Affirmation Set

WRITE THE SECOND FEELING THAT YOU WANT TO CHANGE:

_____

_____

_____

RE-WRITE THE ABOVE STATEMENT WITH MORE POSITIVITY HERE:

(GOOD) _____

_____

_____

DOES YOUR REWRITTEN STATEMENT CONTAIN WORDS LIKE "NOT" OR "I FEEL?" RE-WRITE IT WITHOUT THOSE HERE:

(BETTER) _____

_____

_____

ADD ADJECTIVES AND FEELINGS TO MAKE IT EVEN STRONGER:

_____

_____

_____

RE-WRITE IT ONCE MORE SO IT IS THE HIGHEST LEVEL OF ACHIEVEMENT POSSIBLE:

(BEST) _____

_____

_____

Write an Affirmation Set

WRITE THE THIRD FEELING THAT YOU WANT TO CHANGE:

_____

_____

_____

RE-WRITE THE ABOVE STATEMENT WITH MORE POSITIVITY HERE:

(GOOD) _____

_____

_____

DOES YOUR REWRITTEN STATEMENT CONTAIN WORDS LIKE "NOT" OR "I FEEL?" RE-WRITE IT WITHOUT THOSE HERE:

(BETTER) _____

_____

_____

ADD ADJECTIVES AND FEELINGS TO MAKE IT EVEN STRONGER:

_____

_____

_____

RE-WRITE IT ONCE MORE SO IT IS THE HIGHEST LEVEL OF ACHIEVEMENT POSSIBLE:

(BEST) _____

_____

_____

Write an Affirmation Set

WRITE THE FIRST BELIEF THAT YOU WANT TO CHANGE:

_____

_____

_____

RE-WRITE THE ABOVE STATEMENT WITH MORE POSITIVITY HERE:

(GOOD) _____

_____

_____

DOES YOUR REWRITTEN STATEMENT CONTAIN WORDS LIKE "NOT" OR "I FEEL?" RE-WRITE IT WITHOUT THOSE HERE:

(BETTER) _____

_____

_____

ADD ADJECTIVES AND FEELINGS TO MAKE IT EVEN STRONGER:

_____

_____

_____

RE-WRITE IT ONCE MORE SO IT IS THE HIGHEST LEVEL OF ACHIEVEMENT POSSIBLE:

(BEST) _____

_____

_____

Write an Affirmation Set

WRITE THE SECOND BELIEF THAT YOU WANT TO CHANGE:

_____

_____

_____

RE-WRITE THE ABOVE STATEMENT WITH MORE POSITIVITY HERE:

(GOOD) _____

_____

_____

DOES YOUR REWRITTEN STATEMENT CONTAIN WORDS LIKE "NOT"
OR "I FEEL?" RE-WRITE IT WITHOUT THOSE HERE:

(BETTER) _____

_____

_____

ADD ADJECTIVES AND FEELINGS TO MAKE IT EVEN STRONGER:

_____

_____

_____

RE-WRITE IT ONCE MORE SO IT IS THE HIGHEST LEVEL OF
ACHIEVEMENT POSSIBLE:

(BEST) _____

_____

_____

Write an Affirmation Set

WRITE THE THIRD BELIEF THAT YOU WANT TO CHANGE:

_____

_____

_____

RE-WRITE THE ABOVE STATEMENT WITH MORE POSITIVITY HERE:

(GOOD) _____

_____

_____

DOES YOUR REWRITTEN STATEMENT CONTAIN WORDS LIKE "NOT" OR "I FEEL?" RE-WRITE IT WITHOUT THOSE HERE:

(BETTER) _____

_____

_____

ADD ADJECTIVES AND FEELINGS TO MAKE IT EVEN STRONGER:

_____

_____

_____

RE-WRITE IT ONCE MORE SO IT IS THE HIGHEST LEVEL OF ACHIEVEMENT POSSIBLE:

(BEST) _____

_____

_____

Affirm Yourself

Copy your new affirmation sets to this page

NEW THOUGHTS ABOUT MYSELF: (GOOD, BETTER, BEST)

♡ _____

♡ _____

♡ _____

NEW THOUGHTS ABOUT MYSELF: (GOOD, BETTER, BEST)

♡ _____

♡ _____

♡ _____

NEW THOUGHTS ABOUT MYSELF: (GOOD, BETTER, BEST)

♡ _____

♡ _____

♡ _____

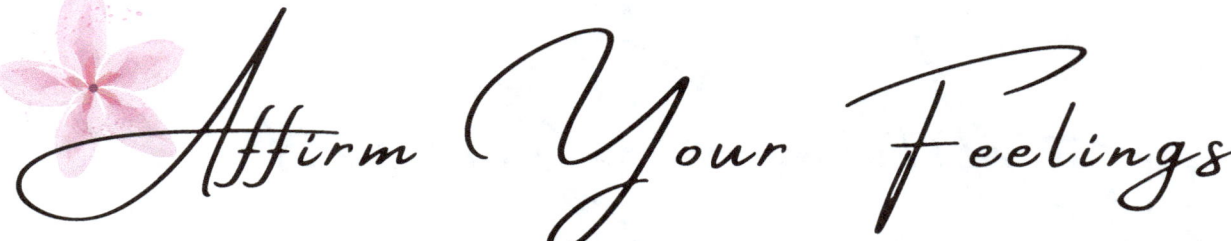

Affirm Your Feelings

Copy your new affirmation sets to this page

NEW FEELINGS ABOUT MYSELF: (GOOD, BETTER, BEST)

♡ _____

♡ _____

♡ _____

NEW FEELINGS ABOUT MYSELF: (GOOD, BETTER, BEST)

♡ _____

♡ _____

♡ _____

NEW FEELINGS ABOUT MYSELF: (GOOD, BETTER, BEST)

♡ _____

♡ _____

♡ _____

Affirm Your Beliefs

Copy your new affirmation sets to this page

NEW BELIEFS ABOUT MYSELF: (GOOD, BETTER, BEST)

♡ _____

♡ _____

♡ _____

NEW BELIEFS ABOUT MYSELF: (GOOD, BETTER, BEST)

♡ _____

♡ _____

♡ _____

NEW BELIEFS ABOUT MYSELF: (GOOD, BETTER, BEST)

♡ _____

♡ _____

♡ _____

Who Are You?

Living as your authentic self means that you remain true to yourself no matter what is occurring around you or with people in your life.

CHARACTERISTICS AND TRAITS OF MY AUTHENTIC SELF: ♡

_____

_____

_____

_____

_____

_____

_____

_____

_____

_____

_____

Who Are You?

Living as your authentic self means that you remain true to yourself no matter what is occurring around you or with people in your life.

CHARACTERISTICS AND TRAITS OF MY AUTHENTIC SELF: ♡

_____

_____

_____

_____

_____

_____

_____

_____

_____

_____

_____

_____

Ask and Visualize

When you're finished speaking your affirmations aloud, it's time to ask for and visualize the things that will contribute to your becoming your authentic self. These include your authentic self's character traits, morals, and skills.

Focus on what you want, not on what you don't want.

Your words, and the focus you put on them,
will make a difference in the outcome.

The previous pages are for making a list of the personality traits, moral convictions, beliefs, skills you desire, and activities that fulfill you. These signify changes that you want in your life because they bring joy, and when you experience them, you feel genuine, authentic, and true to yourself. Some examples of these changes are: being a great conversationalist, a good decision-maker, having an outgoing personality, being a friend that people want, feeling calm and serene, spending time with loved ones, starting new outdoor activities, enjoying peaceful, loving relationships with your children, and accepting and liking yourself.

Visualize yourself doing or having the things you want; relationships, personality traits, morals, beliefs, perspectives, and skills. Ask your higher power for them specifically. Notice how it feels. You have to feel it! What did you observe? If there's inner push-back, I invite you to look closer to discover what the inner resistance means and start working through it.

Give Thanks

Now it's time to thank your higher power for helping you to connect with your authentic self and creating the life you want.

Start by expressing gratitude for everything you have in your life *right now.*

On the next pages, you will create a gratitude list of the things you are grateful for at this moment. Focus on specific people, relationships, events, opportunities, places, and other things for which you are grateful. Be sure to include gratitude for your higher power, your authentic self, and your ability to forgive, love, heal, and nurture yourself. Really **feel** thankful and appreciative for everything that comes to mind. You may notice your vibration intensifying.

Celebrate your wins, and add them to your gratitude list every day. Your list is a dynamic, ever-changing document. Each day and night, refer to your gratitude list and add other things for which you are appreciative: interactions, people, opportunities, transformation, coworkers, clients, family members, friends, pets, neighbors, helpers. Every time you read through your list, you'll notice it's growing, and you'll be reminded that your affirmations are working.

Adding to and reviewing a gratitude list is an enjoyable, vibration-raising way to start each day and finish every evening.

My Gratitude List

I'm grateful for....   because...

_____

_____

_____

_____

_____

_____

_____

_____

_____

_____

_____

_____

_____

_____

_____

My Gratitude List

I'm grateful for....   because...

_____

_____

_____

_____

_____

_____

_____

_____

_____

_____

_____

_____

_____

My Gratitude List

I'm grateful for....   because...

_____

_____

_____

_____

_____

_____

_____

_____

_____

_____

_____

_____

_____

_____

_____

My Gratitude List

I'm grateful for....   because...

_____

_____

_____

_____

_____

_____

_____

_____

_____

_____

_____

_____

_____

_____

My Gratitude List

I'm grateful for....   because...

_____

_____

_____

_____

_____

_____

_____

_____

_____

_____

_____

_____

_____

_____

_____

_____

My Gratitude List

I'm grateful for....   because...

_____

_____

_____

_____

_____

_____

_____

_____

_____

_____

_____

_____

_____

My Gratitude List

I'm grateful for....   because...

_____

_____

_____

_____

_____

_____

_____

_____

_____

_____

_____

_____

_____

_____

_____

_____

My Gratitude List

I'm grateful for....   because...

_____

_____

_____

_____

_____

_____

_____

_____

_____

_____

_____

_____

_____

_____

My Gratitude List

I'm grateful for....   because...

_____

_____

_____

_____

_____

_____

_____

_____

_____

_____

_____

_____

_____

_____

_____

_____

My Gratitude List

I'm grateful for....   because...

_____

_____

_____

_____

_____

_____

_____

_____

_____

_____

_____

_____

_____

My Gratitude List

I'm grateful for....   because...

_____

_____

_____

_____

_____

_____

_____

_____

_____

_____

_____

_____

_____

_____

_____

_____

My Gratitude List

I'm grateful for....   because...

_____

_____

_____

_____

_____

_____

_____

_____

_____

_____

_____

_____

_____

_____

_____

_____

My Gratitude List

I'm grateful for....   because...

_____

_____

_____

_____

_____

_____

_____

_____

_____

_____

_____

_____

_____

_____

_____

_____

My Insights

THINGS THAT I'VE LEARNED ABOUT MYSELF:

_____

_____

_____

_____

THINGS THAT I'VE CHANGED ABOUT MYSELF:

_____

_____

_____

_____

AN "AHA" MOMENT TODAY WAS:

_____

_____

_____

_____

My Insights

THINGS THAT I'VE LEARNED ABOUT MYSELF:

_____

_____

_____

_____

_____

THINGS THAT I'VE CHANGED ABOUT MYSELF:

_____

_____

_____

_____

_____

AN "AHA" MOMENT TODAY WAS:

_____

_____

_____

_____

My Insights

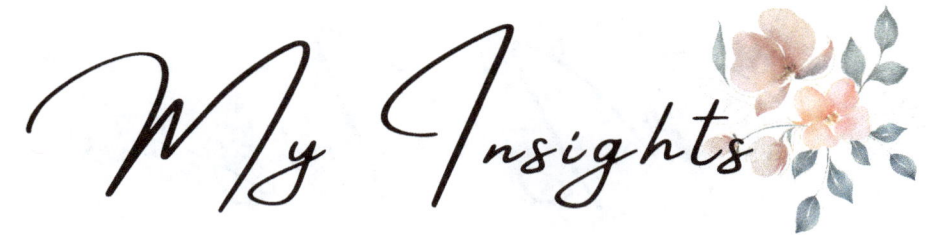

THINGS THAT I'VE LEARNED ABOUT MYSELF:

_____

_____

_____

_____

THINGS THAT I'VE CHANGED ABOUT MYSELF:

_____

_____

_____

_____

AN "AHA" MOMENT TODAY WAS:

_____

_____

_____

_____

My Insights

THINGS THAT I'VE LEARNED ABOUT MYSELF:

_____

_____

_____

_____

THINGS THAT I'VE CHANGED ABOUT MYSELF:

_____

_____

_____

_____

AN "AHA" MOMENT TODAY WAS:

_____

_____

_____

_____

My Insights

THINGS THAT I'VE LEARNED ABOUT MYSELF:

_____

_____

_____

_____

THINGS THAT I'VE CHANGED ABOUT MYSELF:

_____

_____

_____

_____

AN "AHA" MOMENT TODAY WAS:

_____

_____

_____

_____

My Insights

THINGS THAT I'VE LEARNED ABOUT MYSELF:

_____

_____

_____

_____

_____

THINGS THAT I'VE CHANGED ABOUT MYSELF:

_____

_____

_____

_____

_____

AN "AHA" MOMENT TODAY WAS:

_____

_____

_____

_____

_____

My Insights

THINGS THAT I'VE LEARNED ABOUT MYSELF:

_____

_____

_____

_____

THINGS THAT I'VE CHANGED ABOUT MYSELF:

_____

_____

_____

_____

AN "AHA" MOMENT TODAY WAS:

_____

_____

_____

_____

My Insights

THINGS THAT I'VE LEARNED ABOUT MYSELF:

_____

_____

_____

_____

THINGS THAT I'VE CHANGED ABOUT MYSELF:

_____

_____

_____

_____

AN "AHA" MOMENT TODAY WAS:

_____

_____

_____

_____

My Insights

THINGS THAT I'VE LEARNED ABOUT MYSELF:

_____

_____

_____

_____

THINGS THAT I'VE CHANGED ABOUT MYSELF:

_____

_____

_____

_____

AN "AHA" MOMENT TODAY WAS:

_____

_____

_____

_____

My Insights

THINGS THAT I'VE LEARNED ABOUT MYSELF:

_____

_____

_____

_____

_____

THINGS THAT I'VE CHANGED ABOUT MYSELF:

_____

_____

_____

_____

_____

AN "AHA" MOMENT TODAY WAS:

_____

_____

_____

_____

_____

Expressive Writing

Explore new ideas and thoughts here
without censoring or editing

♡ _____

_____

_____

_____

_____

_____

_____

_____

_____

_____

_____

_____

_____

Expressive Writing —

Explore new ideas and thoughts here
without censoring or editing

♡ _____

_____

_____

_____

_____

_____

_____

_____

_____

_____

_____

_____

_____

_____

Expressive Writing —

Explore new ideas and thoughts here
without censoring or editing

♡ _____

_____

_____

_____

_____

_____

_____

_____

_____

_____

_____

_____

_____

Expressive Writing

Explore new ideas and thoughts here
without censoring or editing

♡ _____

_____

_____

_____

_____

_____

_____

_____

_____

_____

_____

_____

_____

_____

Expressive Writing –

Explore new ideas and thoughts here
without censoring or editing

♡ _____

_____

_____

_____

_____

_____

_____

_____

_____

_____

_____

_____

Expressive Writing –

Explore new ideas and thoughts here
without censoring or editing

♡ _____

_____

_____

_____

_____

_____

_____

_____

_____

_____

_____

_____

_____

Expressive Writing

Explore new ideas and thoughts here
without censoring or editing

♡ _____

_____

_____

_____

_____

_____

_____

_____

_____

_____

_____

_____

_____

Expressive Writing

Explore new ideas and thoughts here
without censoring or editing

♡ _____

_____

_____

_____

_____

_____

_____

_____

_____

_____

_____

_____

_____

_____

Expressive Writing

Explore new ideas and thoughts here
without censoring or editing

♡ _____

_____

_____

_____

_____

_____

_____

_____

_____

_____

_____

_____

Expressive Writing –

Explore new ideas and thoughts here
without censoring or editing

♡

Expressive Writing –

Explore new ideas and thoughts here
without censoring or editing

♡ _____

_____

_____

_____

_____

_____

_____

_____

_____

_____

_____

_____

Expressive Writing –

Explore new ideas and thoughts here
without censoring or editing

♡ _____

_____

_____

_____

_____

_____

_____

_____

_____

_____

_____

_____

_____

_____

Expressive Writing –

Explore new ideas and thoughts here
without censoring or editing

♡
_____

_____

_____

_____

_____

_____

_____

_____

_____

_____

_____

Expressive Writing —

Explore new ideas and thoughts here
without censoring or editing

♡ _____

_____

_____

_____

_____

_____

_____

_____

_____

_____

_____

_____

_____

_____

Expressive Writing -

Explore new ideas and thoughts here
without censoring or editing

♡

Expressive Writing —

Explore new ideas and thoughts here
without censoring or editing

♡ _____

_____

_____

_____

_____

_____

_____

_____

_____

_____

_____

_____

_____

_____

_____

Expressive Writing

Explore new ideas and thoughts here
without censoring or editing

♡ _____

_____

_____

_____

_____

_____

_____

_____

_____

_____

_____

_____

_____

Expressive Writing—

Explore new ideas and thoughts here
without censoring or editing

♡ _____

_____

_____

_____

_____

_____

_____

_____

_____

_____

_____

_____

_____

_____

My New Affirmations

Cut out each group of three,
and say them aloud throughout the day

♡ _____

♡ _____

♡ _____

- ✂

♡ _____

♡ _____

♡ _____

- ✂

♡ _____

♡ _____

♡ _____

My New Affirmations

Cut out each group of three,
and say them aloud throughout the day

♡ _____

♡ _____

♡ _____

- - - - - - - - - - - - - - - - - - - ✂

♡ _____

♡ _____

♡ _____

- - - - - - - - - - - - - - - - - - - ✂

♡ _____

♡ _____

♡ _____

My New Affirmations

Cut each group of three,
and say them aloud throughout the day

♡ _____

♡ _____

♡ _____

- - - - - - - - - - - - - - - - - - ✄

♡ _____

♡ _____

♡ _____

- - - - - - - - - - - - - - - - - - ✄

♡ _____

♡ _____

♡ _____

My New Affirmations

Cut out each group of three,
and say them aloud throughout the day

♡ _____

♡ _____

♡ _____

- ✂

♡ _____

♡ _____

♡ _____

- ✂

♡ _____

♡ _____

♡ _____

My New Affirmations

Cut out each group of three,
and say them aloud throughout the day

My New Affirmations

Cut out each group of three,
and say them aloud throughout the day

♡ _____

♡ _____

♡ _____

- - - - - - - - - - - - - - ✂

♡ _____

♡ _____

♡ _____

- - - - - - - - - - - - - - ✂

♡ _____

♡ _____

♡ _____

My New Affirmations

Cut out each group of three,
and say them aloud throughout the day

♡ _____

♡ _____

♡ _____

✂ - - - - - - - - - - - - - - - - - - -

♡ _____

♡ _____

♡ _____

✂ - - - - - - - - - - - - - - - - - - -

♡ _____

♡ _____

♡ _____

My New Affirmations

Cut out each group of three,
and say them aloud throughout the day

♡ _____

♡ _____

♡ _____

✂ ···································

♡ _____

♡ _____

♡ _____

✂ ···································

♡ _____

♡ _____

♡ _____

My New Affirmations

Cut out each group of three,
and say them aloud throughout the day

♡ _____

♡ _____

♡ _____

- - - - - - - - - - - - - - - - - - - ✂

♡ _____

♡ _____

♡ _____

- - - - - - - - - - - - - - - - - - - ✂

♡ _____

♡ _____

♡ _____

My New Affirmations

Cut out each group of three,
and say them aloud throughout the day

♡ _____

♡ _____

♡ _____

- - - - - - - - - - - - - - - - - - ✂

♡ _____

♡ _____

♡ _____

- - - - - - - - - - - - - - - - - - ✂

♡ _____

♡ _____

♡ _____

My New Affirmations

Cut out each group of three,
and say them aloud throughout the day

♡ _____

♡ _____

♡ _____

- - - - - - - - - - - - - - - - - - ✂

♡ _____

♡ _____

♡ _____

- - - - - - - - - - - - - - - - - - ✂

♡ _____

♡ _____

♡ _____

My New Affirmations

Cut out each group of three,
and say them aloud throughout the day

My New Affirmations

Cut out each group of three,
and say them aloud throughout the day

♡ _____

♡ _____

♡ _____

✂ - - - - - - - - - - - - - - - - - -

♡ _____

♡ _____

♡ _____

✂ - - - - - - - - - - - - - - - - - -

♡ _____

♡ _____

♡ _____

My New Affirmations

Cut out each group of three,
and say them aloud throughout the day

♡ _____

♡ _____

♡ _____

✂ ⋯⋯⋯⋯⋯⋯⋯⋯⋯⋯

♡ _____

♡ _____

♡ _____

✂ ⋯⋯⋯⋯⋯⋯⋯⋯⋯⋯

♡ _____

♡ _____

♡ _____

My New Affirmations

Cut out each group of three,
and say them aloud throughout the day

♡ _____

♡ _____

♡ _____

- - - - - - - - - - - - - - - - - - - ✂

♡ _____

♡ _____

♡ _____

- - - - - - - - - - - - - - - - - - - ✂

♡ _____

♡ _____

♡ _____

My New Affirmations

Cut out each group of three,
and say them aloud throughout the day

About the Author

Diane Metcalf is an experienced advocate, speaker, and writer on abuse and family dysfunction. As a result of her own healing journey and continued personal growth, she developed strong coping skills and strategies. She happily shares those with others who want to learn and grow in their own recovery.

Diane holds a Bachelor of Arts degree in Psychology and a Master of Science in Information Technology. She has worked in numerous human service fields, including domestic violence, abuse, eldercare, and developmental disabilities.

She is the author of the highly praised "Lemon Moms" series. This emotionally supportive collection explains maternal narcissistic traits and teaches how to reconcile past hurts, begin healing, and move forward.

Diane's books are a compilation of her education, knowledge, and personal insights regarding her own traumatic experiences and subsequent recovery work.

Currently, Diane writes about recovery from painful relationships by using healthy emotional strategies and tools on her blog, "The Toolbox" (toolbox.dianemetcalf.com).

She currently lives in Nevada with her husband and adorable pets.

This book is intended solely for informational purposes and is not a substitute for professional therapy.

Other Books by Diane Metcalf

1. Lemon Moms: A Guide to Understand and Survive Maternal Narcissism

2. Lemon Moms Companion Workbook: Action Steps to Understand and Survive Maternal Narcissism

3. Lemon Moms Life-Altering Affirmations: Change Your Self-talk, Change YourSELF

All available on Amazon, Audible, Apple Books, Barnes & Noble, Google Play, and wherever books are sold!

Author's Website:
DianeMetcalf.com

Love This Book?

Don't forget to leave a review!
Every review matters!

Your review helps others determine whether this book is helpful.

Head over to wherever you purchased this book and let other readers know your thoughts!

Thank you so much. I appreciate you!